Just as the mighty redwood towers over all the trees of the forest, the saguaro (sa-WAR-oh) is a giant amongst all the desert cactus.

Under ideal conditions, it can reach a height of 50 feet and attain an age of 200 years. When you see a baby saguaro that's only a few feet tall, it's about 20 to 30 years old!

In fact, it will have to survive for 65 to 70 years before it develops it's <u>first</u> branch. So, keep an eye out for all those survivors ... with arms. They are the venerable "senior citizens" of the desert.

Although a mature plant can weigh several tons, the roots of the saguaro cactus are fairly shallow. As a result, strong winds and other natural conditions are a danger, for they are more easily toppled over than any other plant of the same size.

If your travels take you to Southern Arizona and to Northwestern Mexico, you will see their majestic forms dotting the landscapes. Excellent views of dense saguaro forests are presented in the Saguaro National Monument areas of the Tucson and Rincon Mountain units, located on the outskirts of Tucson, Arizona.

Try getting acquainted with these fascinating giants of the desert ... they will both awe and entertain you. Their majesty ... their rejection of conformity ... their occasional way-out human and humorous convolutions ... all <u>talking</u> to each other and, perhaps, to you!

Look at the <u>unretouched</u> photos on the following pages and join in a chuckle at what the saguaros have said to me. Look again! What are they saying to you? Listen ... with your imagination ... and smile as you create a few of <u>your own</u> captions.

Enjoy!

L.M.

Luis Mucciolo

1

"... then, after taking 10 steps, we both turn and fire!"

Your caption: _____

_____

"Mary, don't go! I know what you saw, but it's not what
You think!"

Your caption: _____

_____

"Stop pouting, Junior! Now it's your father's turn at
that computer."

Your caption: _____

"Which way? Well, uh, ... I think, maybe that-a-way!"

Your caption: _____

_____

"Welcome to the lodge, brother member."

Your caption: _____

_____

"Back off, Elmer! I would if I could, but I can't, ...
so I won't!"

Your caption: _____

_____

"Me depressed? No way! It's just the makeup for a new Spielberg sci-fi film."

Your caption: _____

_____

"Please don't force me to choose between you!"

Your caption: _____

_____

"What did he mean ... was I related to Cyrano De Bergerac?"

Your caption: _____

_____

"Okay, kids ... let's move it - it's safe to cross now!"

Your caption; _____

_____

"I know I'm no competition for you-know-who!"

Your caption: _____

_____

"That *#+*#%# mattress threw every one of my discs out!"

Your caption: _____

_____

"I'm the new image for the 'Raise Your Arms' deodorant
TV commercials."

Your caption: _____

_____

"I know you're pregnant ... but. pickles and ice cream
around <u>here</u>?"

Your caption: _____

"Whew! ... I've really had a rough day!"

Your caption: _____

"They said I needed a heck-of-a-lot more than big ears
to be a Playboy Bunny!"

Your caption: _____

_____

"No chance for a lift now, Mabel ... those darn cars got too small!"

Your caption: _____

_____

"Quick, nurse ... the rubber gloves, please!"

Your caption: _____

_____

Robert King

"Everything I touch is fattening!"

Your caption: _____

_____

"Harry, wouldn't it be a better family portrait if you picked the little one up?"

Your caption: _____

_____

"Okay, Okay, I give up! ... Go ahead and invite your mother for a week!"

Your caption: _____

_____

"Did I hear that right? <u>You</u> want to try out for the basketball team?"

Your caption: _____

_____

"They needed a scarecrow ... so I volunteered."

Your caption: _____

_____

"Superman! ... Spiderman! ... and now-w-w-w to the
rescue, it's SAGUAROMAN!"

Your caption: _____

_____

"The doctor said it was perfectly normal if one was a little bigger than the other."

Your caption: _____

_____

"Well, my dear, shall we show them all how to trip the light fantastic?"

Your caption: _____

"Oh, Oh, here she comes now ... let's change the subject."

Your caption: _____

_____

Robert King

"Hey, listen ... I'll give you the wallet, but point that thing away, will ya?"

Your caption: _____

_____

"I don't know why they grew way <u>up</u> <u>there</u> , instead of on my chest!"

Your caption: _____

_____

"Yeah, we're both retired ... worked a long time for the railroad, you know."

Your caption: _____

"Dolly, who ....?"

Your caption: _____

_____

"We're waiting for the Day-After-Christmas sales to start."

Your caption: _____

_____

"Measles? Oh, no! I'm suffering from the golfer's
'hook-and-slice' disease!"

Your caption: _____

"Won't let me drive, huh? Well, you guys don't look
so straight and upright to me, either!"

Your caption: _____

_____

"And, if elected, I promise you ...."

Your caption: _____

"Well, then, someone said, "Off with his head" and before
I knew it ....."

Your caption: _____

_____

"I know garlic is good for a cold ... but <u>not</u> on a date!"

Your caption: _____

_____

"Prolific? ... Yes! But, <u>he</u> doesn't believe in the Pill!"

Your caption: _____

_____

"Okay, buster! Let's settle this thing right now!"

Your caption: _____

"As a child, the 'hanging-tree' made a lasting impression."

Your caption: _____

_____

"Ye Gads! ... What on earth did you do to your hair?"

Your caption: _____

_____

" ... and, even my 'shrink' has been trying to figure
   out who, or what, I am!"

Your caption: _____

_____

"Now, that's touch-dancing, mmm-mmm! Those rock'n'roll
kids don't know what they're missing!"

Your caption: _____

_____

Robert King

"Do – si – do – your partner!"

Your caption: _____

_____

"I was playing in a strip poker game ... and I lost!"

Your caption: _____

"Well, suddenly this coyote jumped into my lap and ....."

Your caption: _____

_____

"This is absolutely the last marathon for me!"

Your caption: _____

_____